# A Hinged Heart

# A Hinged Heart

## POETRY

Jerry Clark

iUniverse, Inc.
New York   Bloomington

iUniverse books may be ordered through booksellers or by contacting:

iUniverse
1663 Liberty Drive
Bloomington, IN 47403
www.iuniverse.com
1-800-Authors (1-800-288-4677)

Because of the dynamic nature of the Internet, any Web addresses or links contained in this book may have changed since publication and may no longer be valid. The views expressed in this work are solely those of the author and do not necessarily reflect the views of the publisher, and the publisher hereby disclaims any responsibility for them.

ISBN: 978-1-4401-8262-4 (sc)
ISBN: 978-1-4401-8261-7 (ebook)

Printed in the United States of America

iUniverse rev. date: 11/16/09

## Hinged Heart

Open to close.
Swoosh!

Closed to open, never.
A one way heart.

# Near Miss

The east bank forever timid
of a mad woman's wrath.
A cruel and heartless whore
Katrina.

Her destruction remains.
Unregulated.
Unfettered.
Will life ever be the same again?

There is no same, no again, ever.

Yet, scant distance west she left
mostly a landscape of damaged roofs covered
temporarily by blue tarps.
Blue-roofs to locals.

West bank dwellers accept
their plight.
A blue roof better than none.
A place to sleep is better than not.

Neighborhoods of houses long and narrow, like northern barges
river floated to New Orleans.
Resplendent in their gaily-painted carnival colors,
standing pride fully under the sea of blue.

Native birds flit about,
cats and dogs remain connected
to their territory.
Perhaps mindful of the near miss.

The near miss, a quirk of nature,
defies logic and reason why only a
sight distant away the bitch
ruled over life, death and entombment.

Today, months later, the haves and have-nots
may not be determined by bank account alone.
Rather by the whimsical path of Katrina,
Or a near miss.

# Today

I have loved you today
in my own way.

The sun greets your face
I seem out-of-place.

Thru the morn
your smile never fades.
I can only see the light scornfully.

The moon sees you true
cast in blue.

I have loved you today
in my own way.

# Words of a Tear

The why will never be
Questioned or Answered.
Words fail more often
Than can be imagined.

Up close I am wordless,
At a safe distance I can refocus.
But
Never will the Tear
Go away, one forever sits
On the rim of my love
For you.

Now, down my cheeks
Tears.
Obstructing view and running free
Always In private.

I know one day, maybe the last day,
I'll shed Pride and release my
Words with the tears.

A partnership ever binding
My love for you daughter.

Until then, words of tears, silent and
Wet upon my cheek will speak,
Only to me.

# Pokies

On my lap rarely
Your gaze meets me fairly.
With eyes older
You become bolder.

Grandpa,
You have pokies
On your face!
Don't you shave?

Eyes gaining higher.

On my lap rarely
Your gaze met me fairly
With eyes older
You became bolder.

Grandpa-finger at my baldhead-
No pokies here!
They're all dead.

Arie

# Old Frank

Old Frank was an onery cuss,
But work he did and well.

Through stubbled field and furrow
he trod straight with head down.
His powerful chest headed forward,
to plowed rows end.

To trod the next row
it mattered not
gee or haw.

Retracing heavy steps a sight to behold
at day's end old Frank filled with pride
and the distance to rest was not far.

The end of day and a barn with
a manger filled with
hay and grain awaited.

If he were a boxer, the weight class
would not be light nor heavy.
A middleweight with
Strong heart would suit him best.

Although, he labored not light
nor middle.
His performance and Herculean effort
could be matched by few.

On the farm Spring was to sow,
Summer the tending,
and Fall the reaping.
This made wintry weather the best.

In winter work is less
only nurturing and hauling wood to burn.
the snow, ice and freezing of day
gives way to barn and warm nights to nod,
then drift to sleep.

Often he was dressed
with buggy harness for a winter's night
ride.
At night Winters Ministry favored all
with silent nights and moonshining's luster.

Pleasing to travel to neighbors door to court,
it was fun to leave trails of hoof prints
and buggy wheel tracks in the snow.
With blanket on back,
head erect with eyes bright
full of deed
and not to plow.

A special place the task determined
with plan for fair that hand.
Driver and sweetheart
would-be hours inside
near the hearth.  Old Frank
quietly waiting contented
for the drivers return.

Into the late winter's night
homeward bound the driver
warmed by his lap robe to slumber
was jolted and brought wide awake.

The borrowed and new
Studebaker buggy was halted
by a wheel hub striking
the Homestead's gatepost.
The driver recovering from sleep

stumbled from the buggy
with lap robe following
to the ground crackling with ice
as it folded itself in a pile.

The driver taking in the scene
noticed first old Frank standing
on three legs with one at rest
and the moonlit buggy shown
brightly like Frank

three wheels clear and one
at rest with its hub caught
on the substantial post.

The driver amazed upon inspection
not a scratch could be found.
A good thing too.

To the front with tender hands
the driver coached the gelding
rearward to free the buggy.

Return to the driver's seat
gave cause to speculate
sleep had overtaken the driver
an old Frank knew the way home.
The only error was turning
to quickly through the Homestead gate.
This slightest bit of resistance
signaled the horse reason to stop.

That night old Frank was stalled,
Rubbed down and the Mr's best and warmest blanket
placed across his back
and a special serving of home-grown
Rich grain for a job well done.

# Thirty and Nine

This morning broke clean
In mid-September.
The puffy clouds over the bay
Look like distant mountains.
This scene today
Is like our
Wedding day, thirty and nine years ago.

We eloped and drove to my promise.
I promised the golden gulf coast.
But gave you a lonely wedding
In a J.P.'s home instead.
Far from your home and family
I gave you a ready-made family with
A two year old.

With style and grace you accepted us.
We were eager to show you our love,
And did.
Later, only months, you embraced
The balance of my family.
A couple of years later we had our
Own family.

Now we were six.
You never faltered, nor failed to pour
Your love into us.
Sometimes we were not as tender to you
As should have been.
We were a family of six soon to be seven.
My aging and childlike father came to us.

# The Library

They, each settled and involved in
Their selections, quietly read side by side.

However, earlier she traveled the
Width and breadth of the sizeable
Space, foraging for the prefect material.
A glossy magazine was brought
To the makeshift nest near the reading
Area of the
Large print section.

Her clothes, mundane and dim, beamed
Of secondary importance.
The white cotton and denim pronounced
No fuss comfort.
Her only indulgence seemed to be
An unlikely hair color.
There she sat
Stopping sometimes, and looking at him.

He, by contrast, is motionless.
Seemingly content
Within the temporary nest while she
Flits about.
His only flourish of movement
Is to turn a page.

Balding and bespectacled
It seems today is a khaki color day.
(Maybe for him each day is)
White socks, displayed with legs crossed
At the knee,
Meet his brown deck shoes.

His choice of reading is a
Hardcover book, complete with
A popular mystery writer's
Picture on the back cover.

Possibly, his reading vicariously
Involves him with dark streets, tainted women,
And murder.

He looks her
Way only when prompted to
Witness a particular magazine
Attraction.
He nods slightly and returns
To the fantasy that is fiction.

Mutually amid the provisional nest
And
Their minds in different places.

A Saturday spent in the library.

I wonder if later
They will host grandchildren,
Enjoy a dinner dock side, or
Return home and never be so
Close again until
The next visit to the library.

# The Eve of 63

Birthday 63.
Past days in May are
Mostly lost to me and
Without details.

A few disjointed remembrances
Can be called to the forefront on
Command.
Like a child's Christmas
Birthdays are markers for material
Selfishness indulging elaborate gifts.

Ashamedly, love ones temporary and permanent
Exist in my minds' fog and are not always
Positioned clearly or timely.

This shame is real to me and echoes and reverberates
As conceit, ego and self-emersion.

Privately, my self's mind oft triggers
A want to return and connect
To memories that are admittedly rearranged
In time and space.
Like drawing a card from a shuffled deck.
(the randomness is an evasion, no need for accuracy)

And like following a rabbits trail throughout the woods
The footprints are endlessly looped to and fro,
A convulsion of steps atop steps atop steps.
My own trail wanders aimlessly about my goal
Of wisdom.

The eve of 63 which me am I?
The me I see
or
The me seen?

In spite of my shameful acts I have been
Remembered, Esteemed, and Loved.
My own trail wanders aimlessly about my goal
Of wisdom.

And why are questions gaining the lead
Leaving answers so far arrear?

63 bears little fruit, little wisdom
And less personal future.
I know there are more birthdays behind than ahead.
Now is my final shot at redemption?

# Halloween

By Arielle

Black cats,
Witches hats.
Flying brooms,
Full moons.

Open the door.
Scare 'em now.
Boooo!

Trick or treat,
Candy please.

**LEEEEEEAVE**

# Sometimes

Sometimes I can
Put a heaping spoonful of
*Swiss Miss* in my coffee
And
Not spill a dram.
Sometimes.

Sometimes I can
Move a filled container from
The fridge to the counter
And
Not spill a drop.
Sometimes.

Sometimes I can
Remove my hot morning oatmeal
With bare hands
Not drop the burning bowl
Sometimes.

Sometimes I can
Bend over to pick up
A penny off the floor.
Sometimes.

Sometimes I can
Stand before
An open pantry
And
Remember why.
Sometimes.

Sometimes I wonder
Why you love me.
Sometimes.

# Small Measures

Life is balanced not by
Large gestures and protracted thought.
Rather living is equalized in Natures' eye
Of small measures.

The first hope of sunrise
To
The last wink of sunset
Reminds us how wonderful
Nature.
And how we are
A grain of sand
On a never-ending beach,
A small measure.

Nature requires communion.
She is never complete.
And
Moves whether we agree
Offering no apology.

Season's first snowflake
Is
A ponderous and silent event.
A soundless promise
Of the last one.
Bound in humility
A small measure.

One breath
Our first
Our last.
A small measure.

# Taxi

Christmas Eve, wish granted,
I'm alone.
The TV and me.
Nothing to do
But stare at the perfect Christmas tree
And the
TV.

Me switching channels
In frantic fashion.
Until
An old and fabulous movie
Of love and separation.
A movie we shared long ago.
Tonight there is no us,
Just the TV and me.

I complete the TV
And come to bed
Only to stare at the open window
And lawn décor beyond.
Minutes pass slowly on the faded clock.
Finally, the inflated giant snowman on
The lawn lies down too.

Here you are and telling the tale
Of your adventure.
How dinner was cold and service
Edgy, like you.
Shoreline of the Mighty River
Lighted to the night
As tradition would have.

Dawn is near, you slumber,
I stare through the window.
An empty taxi slowly passes.
Its driver, like a fisherman trolling,
Looks my way.

He can't see me,
But I wonder
If he could?
Were you not here, I could use a lonely taxi.

# The Clinch

Begin with an introduction,
Quickly move to the first date.

Then, the two find conflict.
Ah!
Resolution is on the way.

Never fails,
At the end they clinch.

# Seldom

Seldom I think not
Of you.

You are to me
Myself and you.

The yoke for two
Must now be born
By only one.

And
Your face filled with
Sunflower blue eyes
And
Sky sunset pink lips
Seldom escape my heart.

Seldom.

# Peaches and Eggs

Surprise me.
Memory reaches to your
Instant reactions, closely held words
Used best at the exact moment
To shrink my poise.

Surprise me.
Then and now I remember
A girl driving a stick-shift convertible.
You at the airport in a Kelly green coat neck to knee-
No match for Irish eyes and flaming hair;
The five-minute dilemma;
Ice cold drink dumped on my head
To cool-off my anger.

Surprise me.
Love me
In astonishing fashion.
My continual struggle to accept
Your entire goodness.

Surprise me.
Years and years
Town to town, across the states
Causing a home to be where a house stood
Before you came.
Surely your bag of surprises of four decades
Must be near empty.

Surprise me.
A Sunday morning,
With near empty cupboards,
You propose the grandest Carte du jour ever.
Peaches and Eggs

# Maybe

Jerry Clark & Friends

Maybe, next time I'll look
First, then leap.
Next time is a second chance,
But with different rules.
Next time is never like the
Last time.
Maybe.

Maybe, listening is better
Than talking.
Listening is like breathing in
Air fresh and clean.
Talking is pollution,
And its output can never be withdrawn.
Never.

Maybe, doing is best.
Tasking from beginning to end
Has rewards.
Doing can be action or thought,
The brain cannot distinguish.
Thoughts are things.
Maybe.

Maybe, the next love
Will be best.
Love of others seldom matches
Love of self.
We redeem self-love often,
Not so often with others.
Pity?
Maybe.

Maybe, roses smell sweeter
Than cherished memory, sweeter than time.
Maybe.
Maybe, time is a beating
Clock on a wall far away.
Maybe.

Maybe, is out reaches was.
Today is yours.

Maybe.

Maybe, life is best and health worthy of
Effort.
Death is not dreaded.
Maybe.

(Leslie)
Maybe, changing surroundings,
Changing clothes, changing people
Is the answer to discontent?
Perhaps self-examination and
Acceptance is the answer.
Maybe.

(KC)
Maybe,
The half-second between sleeping and waking;
The horizon of a new day's dawn,
Will it be bright with the promise of
golden light and brazen breezes?
Or pregnant with the imminent deliverance of torrential rain.
Maybe.

Maybe,
The downy shift of butterfly light lashes
against skin of perfection
A child's innocence luminescent in totality
The utter sheen of love emanating
Will that it always be so;
Or forever driven away by the teenagers right
of passage via obstinacy and pettiness.
Maybe?

# Longest Way

Given to me
As suggest be
Longest way 'round
'tis sweetest way home.

She beyond me
As suggest be
I unproven.

Given to me
As suggest be
Longest way 'round
'tis sweetest way home.

Not sure found
Lingered to bother
But true
Longest way 'round
'tis the sweetest way home.

# Last Second Chance

Living deals the cards and
Sometimes allow a winner.
Second chance is a loser's
Song.

If an other chance
Is allowed, choose carefully.
This second chance
Could be your last.

# January 5

She said, "I want to learn to play!
I've never learned to play!
Maybe once I did?
You?
Have never learned to play either?"

I used to play.
I was a child at home
And
I played a lot!
Play was toys
Like
Trucks, tractors
And
Cars in the dirt.

It seems I did this
For hours
And
My imagination
Prompted my actions.

I could climb trees
And
Look out of my world
From a higher point.

I played
Cowboys and Indians,
Mostly
By myself.


I had enjoyed those times,
It seemed enjoyable,
I seemed peaceful
And
Caught up in the
Play world at the time.

Play?

She is right!
I don't know how to play.

Is it an attitude?
A place?
A time?

How do you learn to play?
Again?
I want to learn.
I want to play,
With her!

# January 13

Clear, cooling.
Yet the cloud of warmth
Stands always close.
Ever close for
Reason
Ever close for
Direction.

Light is clear
Clean
And willing not to
Choke
The spirit.

Stand!
Looking down
And
See how very little
Ground you cover.

Look!
How much is yours?
Property multiplies your
Stance.

Within somewhere there is
A will,
A strength,
That controls and releases unwillingly
To life.

The nighttime is cover
Not allowing perception clearly
Only to see what can
Be
Imagined but not seen.
Trying to hard!

*Hungry?*

*A little.*

*What did you have to eat?*

*Not much.*

*Still having trouble with your feet?*

*Only when it's cold…*
*Bad circulation.*

# Involuntary

Mostly its physical.

Like an eye twitch,
Unannounced and sudden hand cramps.
Nocturnal trips to
Bathroom.

Admiring a pretty woman a
Little too long.
You smile,
She smiles.
She knows no mischief can
Possibly come of it.

Sometimes it's mental.

Private thoughts become public words.
Not to worry.
Your mouth now big enough for
Both feet.

The neutral switch engages
Involuntarily.
Somewhere inside.
You
Know the motor is running
But
The rubber isn't on the road.
Pity?
Not really, you can't remember if
You had anywhere to go.

It's involuntary.

# I Recall

I recall a tiny thing
Born near Resaca's
Where orange trees bloomed
In late November

I recall miles with you
On my shoulders
Not sure of fate

I recall tears from you
And my fears,
We were lonely together

Then you became shared
With one then two and
Many more til less
Of me and more of you

I recall missing teeth
Missing shoes and socks
To quickly missing keys
And stop signs and
Mufflers

I recall Les Paul's in
SLC for your B'day
A Wyoming phone call
To ER-
The last time your tears
And mine mixed.

I recall your flight
To chase your cloud
And how I was not
Of you-
    if ever I was.

Then calls on the phone
Sometimes left a clue
To you but often not-
Family cloth ripped.

I recall not at all
When manhood stood next
To me
Your climb ahead
And mine to down slide.

I recall treks was
Christmas ever for me
Did you take away your sought?

I recall a ceremony
When the world secured
Your promise and so
Became a parting cloud.

Then a stitch missed
But not lost words
Held tongue-tied for
Not knowing the lines.

I recall you becoming
Part of him and he you
Pride in hopes
Of better doing than done.

I recall not enough
To cause a bridge
For you have time to
Child again-
less do I

I recall now you are
Away more than ever
With me and we

Son

# Hoping

Like the rain
Washing my pain.
Your tear
Serves fear.

Like your smile
Cover me awhile.
Your touch
Means so much.

Like you give
I can live
For a time
Hoping you are mine.

# First Fire

Flickering fire.
Flirting fire.
Friendly fire.

Fire, you're famous for
Restlessness attracting
Your next in heart.

Fire, you are famous.

# Diminished

My height is less,
My shoe size greater.
Is this Justice?

My lovers' most intimate and intense acts, only a remembrance
Replaced by a single gentle touch of
Her silken and wondrous lips upon mine

Parenting is condensed to a quite comfortable chair
Out-of-the flow of life, no longer an influence.
No longer an architect of future events.

A shinny novice to new circumstances,
I wonder if soon looking back will
Replace looking forward.

Diminished.

# Cupid Lied

Once, twice, maybe more, cupid
Lied. The lie of one love.
The first began amidst
Life's fluid.

Fabrication closed reasons,
Access bore results to
Crashed arrows.

Cupid lied.

Only to step one
After the other
The sling of arrow's journey sought the mark.

Now finding softer targets,
More stinging without
Recovery or relief.

Cupid lied.

I swallowed hard the taste of
Blood exposed at the entry of a beating spirit.
Again, he found his mark.
I loved often.
Loving struggling
With love.
Never a fixed mark.

Cupid lied.

# My Window

Before my window
dancing ever so carefree,
willing to settle upon
its destiny
The snowflake gives
me
A serenity not
often celebrated.

My window causes me
to ask
Whether I'm moving about
my world
Or
the world moving
about
me?

Either way there is reassignment.
Only I fear
our world,
is moving without
me.

I witness
The journey of a single flake of snow.
Would my touch redirect its path or destroy
the small divine gift?

If I narrow my view
to windowpane size
excluding the world everywhere,

Like touching a snowflake
Can I adjust myself,
into an additional and a greater life,
without ruin?
At least a life that both turns me to myself
And outward to others.

# Constant State

My true love,
Her constant state
Of mind and comportment.

An outcome
Of Nature's tenderness,
And
Elevated values,
Higher than most.

# Cold Waters

Early a day and
halls, benches, nooks
filled with the
he and she and them.

Mumbles turn from chatter,
to profanity.
A clarion announces
the next
case of discontents.

A dissolution of
once common achieving
is now a battlefield,
of distinct hang on to.

The advocates muse
of ifs and ors and maybes.
the ones of decree name are
each buttressed with
family, friends or next one.

Women attract
more bystanders than men,
it seems.
lawyered-up and nervous,
hands shaking and hair astray.

Combatants seek comfort
from cups of caffeine as a
poor substitute for nicotine.
Smiling attorneys, regardless of gender,
openly console while
mentally consulting their checkbooks.

Men's fashion declared with tasseled loafers.
Or western boots for those needing a boost.
All have neckties windowing
the sole.
The women look and smell
of department store buys.
Their footsteps clangorous on tile floors,
the new shoes shinny.
The final gambit before
all credit cards go south.

In these cold waters
the huntress and hunter are fashioned sublimely.
She, either short of skirt or long of dress.
He, suited, starched and sharply creased,
flashing the obligatory Swiss timepiece.
I love to watch the swagger.

Out of the hallways
one by one the weary
of soon to be divorced
disappear into chambers.

Soon, with pledges confirmed,
they exit into the same
halls with the benches and nooks.
a polite shudder of handshakes,
hugs to friends, eye toward the elevator
and freedom.

In their wake
vestiges of
cold waters.

# Child Fathered The Man

Tender and new
the child
Is strong.

Wasted time not to
recover.
Ever.

Slow to succumb,
father transcends
his own childish path.

Child serene.
Hushed witness to change.

The father is self
and
child fathered the man.

# Butterflies of April

Black ones.
Yellow ones.

Orange ones.
Large ones.

Small ones.
All day thru.

They flit wings,
Settle on things.

When people near
They show no fear.

# 1905-2005

Then he was seven.
Now, she is seven.

Tho years measure vastly differs,
Still a tie binds.

I alone bridge the gap.
In one hand the past,
One hand the present.

The future is unknown to each.

The past is ask and be told
By those of then.
My father was seven of a second century ago.

A simpler time on a farm deep in Indiana, populated by
Hard working parents and children.
Spring, summer, fall gave way to work, not schooling.

Winter lay snow deep and warm hearth,
Fire wood harvesting a must.
Inside a candle to light an education,
Outside, beasts of burden resting for spring.

Then Christmas-time,
Without non-stop music of the season.
Without the blitz of commercial TV advertising,
No blinking lights of red and green on artificial trees.

Now granddaughter knows of no need for hard work.
Although parents work hard still,
Seasons differ slightly at the
Gulf Coast and education is public and free.
World wide input available with a click.

Winter and Christmas-time temperate mild for her.
Firewood for decoration cut, split and
stacked at the local grocery.
Inside, school homework via a flood of light
and sparkling computer screen.
Outside, beasts of burden require costly fuel from the pump.
Finally Christmas is near with attendant reds
and greens and retailers hawking wares.
Across the street, puppies for sale.
Expensive natural pine trees from far away
shadowed by speeding passersby.
Limitless choices for shopping lists with
little time to consult sanity.
Perhaps here then and now can be linked?

I am an ignorant connection to he and she.
Had more questions been asked and most important,
Answers heard. Who knows?
Too busy for my own and now not wanting to fail with her.

If I asked "how was Christmas for you?"
He would have answered an answer I'll never know.
How did he build a rabbit trap from barn scrap wood?
He did teach unasked for knowledge.

Spotting a squirrel high in a pecan tree on a windy day,
By sighting the slightest movement of its tail as the body
Remained controlled and still.
I did not learn how to guarantee a lasting fire or hunt ducks.

She knows nothing of his Christmas or mine.
Is she burdened of my past holiday, unknowing?
I skipped a generation due to unworthy opinion of time spent.

One hundred years separate the seven year olds.
Are attempts then and now are ever going to connect the two.
Perhaps this Christmas.

# 5 Minutes

"…Houston flight will begin
Boarding in 5 minutes."

"5 minutes to decide," she said.

Not to watch her,
I turned to see
A bank of pay phones
Being robbed.

5 minutes, I thought.
Not long enough
Or
Too long?

The decree read
5 minutes to freedom,
Or married life.

Life it was to be.

Gladly, life it is.

# To Choose

Wise to world's time,
people develop.
Some straight, some bent.
But all choose.

# Now 64

For me, each year passing is marked
By a day.
My birthday.
The only day of the year
That's mine.

Evidence of transient life cycles,
Touching my obscured life.
Measuring my day
Versus others.

Now, 64.

My being is now unrestricted.
Sound medical purveyors
Are at heel.
Percentages of ill health given without drama

The uniformed face of each
Wears the disguise well.
Fortified with intelligence,
Exams and prognostications,
First one than another offers
Counsel regarding different parts of me.

"Your heart function is worsening, less than 30%-difibulater?"
"Your kidney function is 70% gone-dialysis is next"
"Yours diabetes is uncontrolled-insulin injections"
"Sleep-You stopped breathing 100 times in an hour-CPAP?"

Pragmatic souls all.
Goodly intended, armed with the limitations
Of their learning.
Marking the rally
To my end

With their saddening songs.
I hear, sometimes see them. I
Become most familiar with the wait.
And
What about me?
Me.
Laying in the back seat of a new 1949 sedan
*Windows open, staring at summer clouds.*
*Miles to travel.*

*Family summer vacation begins.*

However, if that were the only news
It would be time for sad songs and
Slow singing.

While clawing out of this
Me shell, discoveries
Are made or remade.

My love, my wife is tireless
And unrelentingly at hand
With the next pill, the next medical
Appointment, the next smile and touch.

Family looks on in discomfort,
But I hear none
Of their obligatory hospital hallway whispers.
So, life remains at hand.

The future, of some measure, is in the wind.
To learn and apply knowledge apart
From self-interest.

I remain loved and honored by family,
And personally hopeful in the year ahead.
All the while, I am dedicated to finding
That place called Happy.

# Periwinkle

Blue-lavender carpets
The soil
Closely held, best in shade
Yet seasonally springs in soft colors of pale blue.

Like some who thrives in shady
Shadow-adding much
Tint and softly embracing their
Environment.

If there were no sun of love
There could never be shade.

# Plastic

Hospital bound, time to squander,
I look around.
Hallway, every nook and niche,
Garbage bags, sandwich bags,
Body bags.
Plastic.

Surgical tubes,
Newborn beds.
Janitor's bottled cleaners, mop pales,
Feeding trays, spoon and fork,
Plastic.

Hanging plants, a ficus in the corner
Care giving
Not required.
Tender nurturing of nature
Absent.
Beauty without substance
Not living or dying.
Plastic.

Beverage, food containers
And toilet seats bent
To obey the rules of the
Designate moneychangers.
Plastic.

Glint or stare the world is awash,
Doomed perhaps.
Board a ship or fly the world
Bury the dead.
Leave the human blunder to
Plastic.

# Sisters

The oldest a delicate reed,
To sing songs
And
Speak volumes with her eyes.

The youngest vibrant,
Needing to be seen while seeing.
Nothing escapes her view.

Together a duet
Of delight and charm.
The first solitary,
The second a-team of one.

Together they are
Treasured Granddaughters.

# The Golden Year

Here it is.
Retirement.
The year of the entitlements,

*"Oh, look, my Medicare card."*
First-rate times are
Around the bend, on every street.
Senior discounts.
Respect from the young?

I ask
What's left to
Do?
To see?
Only the remains of
My life on black and white celluloid
Flickering giantesses on darkened walls
Of my drollness.

The occasion is marked with
Mail for this and that.
It's a kind of congratulations
Coupled with the presumption
I'm easy fodder for scams.

What is not in the junk mail is how
To go from here to the
Unknown conclusion.

One fixation is clearer today than ever
Before in my spirit.
My bond with
My lover, my wife, my Nancy.
Mentor of life's real
Worth.
Love.
She is convincing me
I'm worthy.

Never will know where a different
Pathway may have brought me,
But I'm lucky enough to
Have this one.

# The Last Clark

This is your Family Tree.
All trees have limbs
And branches,
So do the Clark's.

Countless Clarks have preceded you.
Let's meet a few of them.

In 1775
Daniel Boone,
As a frontiersman and Indian fighter,
Blazed the Wilderness Road to Kentucky.
And later became a politician from Virginia.

In 1776,
His cousin,
George Rogers Clark;
A Revolutionary War soldier,
Fought with George Washington.

His nephew,
Captain William Clark,
Of The Lewis and Clark Expedition,
Mapped a trail to the Pacific Ocean.

In 1919,
My father, a Great-Great nephew,
Came to Oklahoma to work in the
Booming oil fields.

In 1943,
My brothers and your
Great uncles
Carl, Kenneth, and Harold Clark,
Fought in World War II.
Harold, a sailor, lost his life in the Pacific.
A university student.
And today you are the last branch
On my Family Tree.

# The Spring of 66

Years overtake, days collected to no account known.
Of all I know each day and year seems indifferent
But somehow are becoming the same.

Aging is Nature's way of rebuilding itself in others
Near you and full of what has offered itself of you.

Yesterday is today and today wonders
what happened to yesterday.
A puzzle of little clue and often no answer revealed
Lacking the attention and focus to maintain discovery.

Life's moments are filled with wonderful tones of voice
Spelled lovingly from family.

Rambling of deeds and direction fail to dictate the goal
Of the moment.
No matter, the Advent predestined as if ordained.

# What If?

What if you love
But resist
Speaking it?

As a child, true innocent
Love is expressed
Continuously.
From the first vocal
Expression of making bubbles,
Cooing with infant lips.

The child grows taller,
Knees shining through pants,
Elbows skinned
Courtesy of the last bicycle wreck
Cannot seem to get the words out.

Yet on Mother's Day
And Father's Day
Hand made cards
Expressing three little words.
I love you.

Older and much taller
They falter nervously
To speak the same three words.
Not only to parents,
But often, to their true love.

This communication breach
Stuck between the 20s and 50s
When love is not spoken, rather
trinkets and flowers
Becomes the exchange rate.

What if?
At the finale the only medicine
To comfort is to say
I love you?

What if?
As Air

Your loving breathe to satisfy my empty self.

Eyes reflecting mountain trees and dancing lemon colored leaves
Seal my only truth.

Generously given, you fill my space,
As air.

# Smile

Smile, and when you do
Your doubts are forgotten.

Smile, and when you do
Your fears are forgotten.

Smile, and when you do
Your hopes are here to
Stay.

Smile and when you do
Your best never goes
Away.

# Thursday, Again

If it were Thursday again,
Friday would be next
with its promises.

The promise of joy and relief
of a week past and next
week to distant to matter.

The promise of altering patterns
of loving and renewing dreams,
the week end begins.

From the bridge of Thursday
Friday creeps into view
and
sensory dreams turn to
celebration and glee.

For practiced eyes if
Friday's horizon is seen
one can force future
realities-even so far
as Saturday and Sunday,
but never Monday. that
flag is not unfurled.

Thursday again is welcome.

For one time Monday came
too close, too soon.
its arriving announced as if
by prophecy of heretics
and non-believers
standing tall, their shadows
increasing.
darkness.

A She-Devil,
Wrought horror.

Heaven denied, New Orleans soiled and rancid.
Ensuing reported words meaningless.
Flicker by flicker TV images unfathomable.

If it were Thursday again,
Friday would be next
with its promises.
not
Monday, not yet.

Monday a day tears
became torrents never ending.
Hurricane Katrina-
A Monday in August, 2005

# Nature Happens

Sunrise, yellow daffodils, and floods some of
Nature's best and worst occur without measure.

Nature heeds no measurement, it simply does.

However.

Humans must measure everything-know the precise
time of a sunrise, how many flowers and why yellow?

Numbers must quantify natural disasters;
song lyrics ask how high the moon.

In general, we humans labeled everything, and nature
could care less. Our character is boundless and we have
maintained our arrogances across time and place.

Including meddling with Nature via cloning plants and animals.

# Hard Wired

You can go wireless,
you can be creative,
but unless you are
hard wired you are
a cheater.

# Leaning

Man walks upright
unlike lower forms,
yet is most heartfelt
when leaning.

Although man clicks
to travel worldwide,
He leans to the screen beseechingly.

Religious devoutness has man
leaning in submissive prattle.

Sorrow and all misery accepts
leaning for the curative.
We are joined regardless of
language or culture.

Leaning surrenders the pretense
of
Sincerity.

# A Skinny Geranium

Aging, thin and minus past
flourish
a
Skinny Flower,
long of stem, short of bloom
proudly presents
its best.

The stem of beauty
crescents in red petals.
If
examined closely
reveals past glory,
Resplendent.

Unknowingly, its best is gone
with season past.
A single refugee
from the potter's shed.

A skinny Flower knows
not its decline.
It knows only Nature
demands production,
demands life on a stem-
life on display.

Aging, too thin a stem,
too little a flourish of bloom,
Yet
is the most delicate of Nature's best.
A skinny Geranium.

# Table Four

She is coy.
He, disinterested, at first.
a lovers language heard and spoken?

However,
my witnessing the café
scene I saw what he could not.

Beneath the table her naked feet
are dallying with summer sandals.
Her legs, uncovered by the brief hem of a summertime dress,
disappear above the edge of the linen table cloth
and are
constantly in motion .

In contrast, he sets aim on his
luncheon sandwich
And is
Motionless-save a word or two
between bites.
Under the table his
expensive tasseled loafers show
beneath his properly creased
trouser legs.
Each shoe is unmoved and perfect looking.
Wait, he moved his legs to repose them
And
between his shoe and pant leg
I see out-loud in my face-argyle socks!
(personal favorite of mine)
Is he a player after all?

Above table four her body is erect and calm
taking notes on a note pad.
All the while, the dance below continues.
The performance, seemingly staged,
held no apparent insight to future events.
How could they?
He is clueless to the rejoicing of nude feet and bold hemline.
A dance of intent never seen.
"Is everything ok"?
The waitress asks.
He nods politely.
The waitress takes note
To share the scene with
The kitchen.

I begin to feel the intruder
Of a private event in a public place.
I turn away.

Later, by accident, I look their way
to see her touching his hand.
Professionally.
Now, I notice the dance of his loafers quickly
betrays
his stoicism above the table.

I check my watch and it is
Time for me to go.
I may never know the outcome
Of
Table four.

# Temporary

everyone is temporary,
You will never be.
in my heart you will
be all that's never wary.

Everyone is temporary
we are told.
in my heart you will
always be to hold.

everyone is temporary
You will never be.
in my heart's place
you are forever with me.

# Littleness Two

hardly to notice
the
littleness of life.

to look not,
but
to see
believingly.

youth's no episode
to learn.
they desire the
solitary swim of
the giant torrent.
struggling, striving self-interest.
blind to all littleness.

young looks not
defining terms outside
their self-wasting.

then,
mid begins.
only to support failing
youthful wishes.
remaining fettered, floundering
unforgiving
and failed in the
littleness of life.

troubled relics
of
looking not
seeing.

odd, we seem not able
to glean details-for
details are often smaller
than life-not for the imp,
rather for the unsaid.
age sees messages in
slightness and dust
hovering in a meaningless way.
seeing love
where
words never go.

love.

youth is a bleeding vessel.
sudden starts, quicker endings
leaving
only a turned cup.

mid longs to rekindle
glory, filling life a blur of
scenery.
now, flurry of drama
falls not to notice
other than themselves.
shame.

like youth,
mid dance
partner-less,
unmindful of
most talented
and
eager shadows.

age, not scores of numbers,
sees
imports not disport
filling the cup
gracefully.

mindful of monotonous
youth and mid.
age smiles esoterically.
one time,
yet
to see
change will travel resonantly.

although destination worthy,
age travels sounding of
shut memories.
not of glory
or blood rush.
rather, of
small things
to see
where words never
to be found.

littleness
of
love.

# Educated and Duped

Best I remember
he was young, bespeckled,
and educated.

As the fabrication
Plant Engineer
Of special vessels with severe
specifications and construction.

As constructors ourselves
we were installing new equipment
high above ground level.

The Plant Engineer was always nearby
when our mobile cranes
were working.
Our foreman would chat
with him between lifts.

Our man convinced him
the cranes would not move
unless he provided certain
hand signals.

The amusing part was
our man told him
that our company insured
his hands for $1 million.

The crew discovered how
easily the young educated
Plant Engineer would take
anything that they said as gospel.

I remain uncertain
if he ever knew.

# 44 Years Today

44 years old today,
Do I know where my son is?
Not for years.

Birthdays past
Were events for our oldest child,
Our firstborn.

As the gifts and applause
Showered down, he always smiled
Charmingly.
Always a thankful recipient.
My guess is he hasn't changed much.

Like they must, he grew up
And flew away.
On his own, behavior mostly good,
Became tainted.

Honorable deeds sprinkled
With misdeeds.
Some criminal.

Redemption always a fleeting
Gossamer.
The allure of money and praise powerful,
Too powerful for some.

Today, a checkered past,
A broken family, the charming man
And son-where ever you are
A birthday wish- find harmony and peace.

I love you son.

# 50 Years Ago

1957 life was good.
I remember it well.
Cars had fins, lots of chrome,
And the Edsel was a new.

Gasoline plentiful and cheap,
Milk was original and abundant.
Trends in pink and black.
TV replacing theaters,
A King named
Elvis.

High school styles of blue jeans,
White t-shirts, sleeves rolled up.
Head topped with duck tales
With Old Spice hair wax.

And.

Her style complete
Poodle skirts and handbags matching,
Bobby socks
And penny loafers.

Drive-in restaurants served
10-cent Cokes.
Saturday spent polishing the family car
For a Main Street parade
Later.

Life was good
50 years ago.

Then came Sputnik I.
I remember it well.

# Bedroom by the Kitchen

The aroma of breakfast
Of biscuits and bacon.
No need to call my name.
I'm awake, mouth watering.

# Easy Absence

Neither the first, nor the last
Is easy to say good-bye.
In between find the easy absence.

Like parents watching the school bus
Disappear around the corner.
And later reappear around the same corner.
In between find the easy absence.

Spouse at the airport walking away, then
A plane wheels-up over the runway.
The knowing leaving is a part of returning.
Still, many partings are labored and not easy.
Remember.

Neither the first, nor the last
Is easy to say good-bye.
In between be thankful for an easy absence.

# Eight More Days

Eight more days he'd be twelve
Years old.
Often a tough age
For a boy, especially at school.

Puberty, locker room jokes,
Some boys are taller,
Some are shorter.
Some voices are deep,
Some voices squeak.

Boys are challenged daily
With sports, academics, hallway or
School bus bullies.

For some, not all, the bright spot
Of the day is returning home.
At home, in their room, some seek refuge
In violent and graphic games
Seen in videos, movies and TV.

Often acting-out this violence
Leads to disaster outside the home
And sometimes within.

Eight more days he would have been
Twelve Years old.

# Fallen Bloom

For weeks I've enjoyed
Our Orchid plant showcased
Proudly on the dining room table.

Today, under that plant
I saw a fallen bloom
Laying so still, yet beautiful,
But alone.

Its companions
Remained, adorning
Branches so thin and fragile.

I thought how like people.
We don't truly miss them
Until they become
An exquisite
Fallen Bloom.

# Footfall

A strand of memory
Remains core deep in my self.
Just began as infant fixed in place
Without movement or travel of space,
Hears the footfall of parent leaving away
Out of a room.

No control of departure, or clue of return.
A child given bed at night and held prisoner
To a vault of cloth and leather shoes.
Shoes immobile til the morrow.
Still can hear footfalls away.

Angered spouse out a door away.
Footfall and door fall silent with her passing,
No sign of next time or if next is possible-
Footfall away.

Lost to my self the line is drawn and I shall not pass.
Out of sight silence of absence.
Sterile of ill and infirm sorted like laying hens
in spaces with doors and screens lend only what
can be heard-footfall advancing, sounds
Of nurse shoes dreaded.

Welcome their footfall away without me.
Not me today to down the hall. Like an infant fixed in space
Still, worse with selfish to life-heart
breaking when footfall away of
My love.

# Going to Happy

Through that gate over there
Just past the playground,
Passed the carousel
You'll find your way.
Your not lost, stop and look
Around.

See the flowers full of bloom
And soap bubbles that
Go boom.

Short breeches, skinned knees,
And too many summer freckles are allowed.
Go on.
Happiness is on the other side
Of a sweet tasting little creek
With
Comfortable steeping stones
To cross on.

There is plenty of sun or shade
Along the way.
Go ahead.

Happy is a journey
Or a destination?
No matter-
The reality is you are
Looking for Happy.

Come on,
Take a peek
Through that gate over there.
Just past the playground...
Go ahead.

# Gumption

Gumption has no moral compass.
History is filled with famous
And the infamous that have displayed
Gumption.

George Washington had it,
So did Bonnie and Clyde.
Hitler had gumption.
The original Astronauts had gumption.

Gumption is an informal noun.
Resource books use synonyms
Such as, intellect, energetic, shrewd,
Common sense.

Is it innocent?
And without consequence?
What does the intellect, the energy,
Common sense, search for?

Most agree and
Accept action often generates reaction
And often produces a circumstance or consequence.
One must take responsibility, even for the bad.

Is that it?
Corporate America may be the worst.
We can no longer find or identify
The responsible person.
Everyone seems to pass the buck.
Remember, Harry Truman said,
"The buck stops here."

Think back to childhood,
Good deeds were rewarded,
Bad ones punished.
Gumption had a moral compass.

Now, as adults
Are all brains
Regardless of ethnicity,
Religious belief, sex, and even age
Cross-wired to believe
Any action that suits us
Is okay?

If you had gumption today-
Where does your moral compass indicator point?
I leave you the question.

# I Hate Saturday Mornings

Saturday mornings are riff with
Moans, groans and wishes for more sleep.

About Six AM, the girls find breakfast
Through half closed eyes, eat
Fiercely amid grumbles
Of why am I doing this/that?

Dad, the cook, answers-
Because you love it.

Moms and girls out the door, down the driveway
The family wagon packed full of
Stuff.

Down the street and over the bridge
They go.

Hatred starts turning
To something like-
Wow.
No traffic, no hand signals
From grumps on the six-lane.

On to the rendezvous quietly
But for the switching of radio stations.
Saturday Mornings are ripe
With info-commercials, not music.

Our Friends, trainers-our Saturday morning family awaits.

At the stables these kin gathers
For the love, the pleasure and
Bonding with horses.

Horses of many
Colors, backgrounds
And skill levels.
Each one proudly brought to shine by grooming brush.

All are readied, some with English tack, some
Western, all set for equestrian training.
Moms, daughters, granddaughters
Gathered by the common love
Horse and riding.

A time
For girl freedom, apart
From the kitchen, homework,
School or office pressure,
Just gals and horses.

I love Saturday Mornings.

# Linesider

The Wild West, famous for its
Fighters.
Comanche, Apache, and more.
The men and boys in Blue
Who fought them.

The natives skillful and
Fearless.
Ready to prove their cunning
And superiority.

The Military with meager outposts,
Manned by fresh young and untested leaders
Supported by crusty life-timers.
Both fodder for real fighters.

However, a common craving linked them.
Like jousting knights of long ago,
They loved a fight, a contest to uphold
Their honor, to prove superior
To a rival.

That was then.
Today,
Men anguish over being
A skilled player-a good fighter.
Still untested professionals, Doctors, Lawyers,
Wall Street pundits rely on
Crusty lifers to point the way to a good fight.

Looking for glory and reason to pound
Chests that only  winning a struggle can produce.

What do they do?
Where do they go?

They go fishing.

Not only do they fish,
Often great monies are exchanged
For travel, lodging, and of course
Those resident experts
Who know the waters
And
The prizes within.

Sometimes, not always, a
Prize catch is brought to bay
With proof offered via
Photographs.

Not to be remiss in this
Chronicle, the stories-fish stories-
Often the most memorable,
Lend a personal touch
Back home where
Perhaps the big catch
Is embellished if not immortalized.

Maybe the best of the best
Is a story of
Walking a fish, like walking a dog,
To the above mentioned photo opportunity.
The photo is one thing, but to hear the story
Is an experience not forgotten.

# Still

Still, standing before
The door of what
Is yet to be,
My heart beats
Excitedly.
Perceptions of life's mystery begins
Womb bound,
With time alone to ponder.

Then, into the human race a
newborn in a hurry to be
Adult.
Not knowing its future,
Not even the next moment.

Still, plans are made and implemented
As if to control events
Obscure in every corner.

Still, we plot and plod
Blindly to the next ambiguity
As to maintain
The sanctuary of our destiny.

Still, a fool full of hope standing
Before the door of what is yet to be,
My heart beats
Excitedly.

# Manicure

Ever notice the complete
absence of thought
when manicuring your fingernails?

I'm a guy that cares for
his own fingernails
and always have.

Just today, sunlight streaking
across my desk,
I realized there was work to do
on my fingernails.

Reaching in the cluttered drawer
for my old and favorite
nail clippers I went to work.

Minutes later I complete my task
and admire my work.
During this personal time
I cannot recall a single thought
beyond my nails.

How about you?

# Never Did

Never did pilot a 10 second
Hot Rod down the drag strip.
Never did swim with fish,
A scuba tank on my back.

Never did solo an airplane
High in the sky.
Never climbed a mountain
To the top.

Never saw a lighthouse beacon
From the deck of a ship.
Never did go to the moon.
Never did go to war.

Never did tell Mom and Dad, my kids
I love them often enough.
Never told my lover-best friend-wife
The same.

Never did tell
The entire truth
Of me.

Today, I
Celebrate with wife and family
Forty years of matrimony.
Can you say that?

I just did.

# The Fedora

In the day, a phrase offered
From the aged to youth,
Is known to mean: look back.
To repeat was, ignoring is.

Good times and bad can be found
In the past, it's the same today.
Its the same today save one universal
Feature, the Fedora.
That soft felt hat so popular in the 40's and 50's.

USA, Europe, (in Britain known as the Trilby), all over.
The Fedora,
Felt in winter, straw in summer,
A hat no man refused,
Its broad snap-brim pulled low over
The eyes, the silken band wide,
Often with feather, and
Showy accented the vertical crease
Separating the pinched crown.

Everyone wore their version,
Like a good 3 dollar guitar
It was affordable to all.
So fixed it was removed only inside
Or during the depression of the 20's
When it became a convenient coffer for street
Corner and gutter beggars.

Mystery still surrounds the Fedora.
One question remains.
When at what age did a young man
Visit the haberdashery for his first?

More important, Hollywood
Made hat fashion a noir icon.
Cops, Private eyes (even Dick Tracy and his
Yellow fedora), criminals and such.
A fedora and trench coat was the uniform
Every man, woman, and child
Understood.
But wait!
How did the guys kiss the gals,
With snap brim low on the face?
Did the guy wrangle such an arrangement?
The meeting of lips was possible?
Lo, does he remove his symbol of manhood
Revealing his intent?

Such tension recognized and dispatched by
The same movie moguls that gave
Birth to the symbol buried it.
Hollywood single handedly
Transported the hat from the darkened
Alleys with hat on,
to
Brightly lighted stages.
No fedora

But, still, real actor men needed
Distinctiveness.
In with wavy hair,
And thin mustaches
And square jaw lines
The camera loved all three.

Three to replace one image.
Hooray for Hollywood.

# Sunday, West Beach

Sunday at west beach
Unseen forces work
As gulf waters meet
The sand.
Each wave demanding completion.

All
Waves persistently, rhythmically
Approach the isle.
Their journey ended.

Like surf driven
To meet sand.
I am driven to you.

Each wave is steady, faithfully
Goes ashore.
Knowing it will be replenished
Day by night by day
The surf continues endless.

My love is the same, never ending
As I choose you, forever.

# Snow

Snow is the heavens best gift.
Snow
Covers, clings, cleans,
Displays newness and desires smugness.

Snow is
Patient waiting to be received.
It requires nothing or
Demands everything.

Man must know
Snow mutes thought,
Considers appreciation,
Fondness and wooing.

Snow is
Man's rebirth.
With snow there is only the present,
The past covered
And
Future un-plotted.
Only now, the height of awareness is present.
Opportunity is seized to right wrongs.

Selfish?
Is not the apparition
Snow gives
In its own way clinging
By the same?

Softly touching.
Falling, jointly with
Its kind until
Pure and innocence
Can no longer be denied.

Its depth seldom known
Until tested cautiously
Not wanting to be enveloped with
No standing.

However, developing (setting the stage)
And
Upon invitation
Snow
Can trust upon what it
Builds.
Thus contented in its own release
Without fear.
Please! Snow!

Presence of snow can
Either be
A whisper or
A complete rage:
Depending.
I love snow.

When spotlighted snow answers
Brightly and immodest.
The eye cannot deny its shine.
Snow!

Watch it happen, know it
Cares.
Share, accept the offering.
Penetrate and search snows
Essence
And

It will respond hungrily.
Accepting your desire once,
Twice and more.

Its reaction to my action,
To each step, leaves a mark.
Yet ahead no signs.
Does snow only react?

So long as I embrace
The heavens it will snow.

# Passerby

Once, then again,
I take in every detail
As you walk by.

Your height, your stride
Your fragrance.

I do not speak,
I hoped that you might.
You did not.

Once, then again,
You walk by.
I take in every detail.

Overlooked by you.
I remain silent.

# Just There

Just there near your
Ear.
The rewards show per year.
Silver threads shine when
Near.

Never to show, even to
Fear.
Just there near your
Ear.
Silver threads shine when
Near.

# Dawn of 66

Dawning is as much ending
Night as is the beginning of Day.
To witness the passing night
Is to recount events, the process
Of gaining the glow.

Lessons learned project themselves
Into the flaming red and orange ribboned and
Knotted as life itself in the
Morning sky.

Dawning of a new time
Lends to mans brush stroking clean
Waning history.

Those choosing times gone by
Do so as not to toil with hope in the heart.
Today yearns to be molded and created
Becoming tomorrows past.

# It's Summertime

Walking down a gravel road
Kicking stones, practicing your spitting,
And chasing grasshoppers that cross your path.
They'll be fish bait later on.

When barefoot early day is best
Before the sand and gravel roads get hot.

Destinations are important early in the day,
Like a friends' house or the local country store,
Where a bag of salty peanuts and a bottle of RC cola
Can be yours for 25 cents.

Learning is a part of summer, like pouring
Peanuts into RC cola, shaking it to fizz.

Now, you can drink
And eat one handed.
Perfect when riding your bike.

The same bike now
Makes a throaty noise like a motorcycle.
Simple to do with
Dad's best poker cards secured
With Mom's new clothespins.

Mid day is hot and time for a swim,
Country style-

No clothes in the neighbor's farm pond-
The same pond the annoying hand-sized Perch
Stole the mornings grasshopper bait collection from
Your only fish hook.

Finished your swim and quickly retreating
To your clothes and the next
Adventure.
First you stop at waters edge.
And enjoy the sense of
Cool red mud between your toes.

That nearby old tree with low swooping limbs
And frequent knots offer a toehold.
Such a tree is made for kids and climbing.

You sit in a limb fork of a high limb,
Watching the mud dry between your toes.
Wet hair press to the tree and eyes closed
You are keen to sounds of the tree.

Insects buzzing, leaves silently turning in the breeze
You hear the tree itself
Celebrating full bloom, proud to offer
Cooling shade to whomever stops by.
The natural symphony sounds its
Lullaby and you nap.

You awaken and the heat is
Gone.
As you meander home.
The cooling evening is
Producing its show.

The first twinkling of a star and the rim
Of a shallow moon.
The best are the
Much closer lighting bugs with their flashing neon bodies.
You've heard of a boy, like you, catching so
Many he filled and lighted a Mason jar.
Just so he wouldn't be afraid in the dark.

So many sights, so many new sounds.
You hear a far-off sound.
Mom is calling you to supper, bath and bed.

You speed home with thoughts
Of the day and dreading the next.
Until you remember there is no
School tomorrow.

*Schools out, schools out,*
*The teacher let her mules out.*

It's Summertime.

# I Dared

Once I dared
To stop
And
Look.

What I saw was a
Shadow
Cast upon the ground.

If I moved
So
Did the shadow.

I did not move
Nor did it.

When the sun sets
The shadow
Becomes completed
Within its own world.

No longer a stranger
Needing
Its object to provide shape.
But
Rather it is free,
To mingle,
To search,
To move about
Indolently
Steps taken
But
No trace.

Footfall with not
A sound.
Eyes opened
Or Closed
The night cares not.

Shadows care not.

# Homemade

Summer at my house was filled
With activity
None better than consuming spoon full
After spoon full of
Homemade ice cream.

That cold ice cream
Was always best on the Fourth of July
Always a family event.

When I was born my older brothers
Were a fighting war.
The youngest of them never returned from the Pacific
He was born on the Fourth of July.

Do parents ever get over it?

So, the family always gathered at my
House for a day of Summer fun and
Remembering.

The women collected around my mom
In the house
While us "men" collected around dad outside
Under the best shade tree ever.

Us men would surround the object
Of my attention
The ice cream maker
A wooden artifact with a mechanical
Crank.

The process of making ice cream
Was mostly lost on me
I did understand cranking was
Vital.
Turns cranking were taken by all the men
As they discussed important
Issues of the day

Whatever?
Not to interrupt my elders I was
taught,
But crept ever closer
To the device.

Summers passed and I grew
to cranking size, I hoped.
Surely this would be my Summer!

The day came finally
An older brother extended
An invitation to crank.
A nod of head really

Now in the circle I was centered
The hub I had longed to be
Everyone about me smiling
The smile of welcome.

Especially, my dad and hero brothers
Were watching me
I sat in the rickety lawn chair
The throne of ice cream making importance

Grasping the handle
Feet planted as I had seen
I Smiled in return
My effort to crank
Was met with not a budge!

Again, bettering my grip,
My best efforts were met with no movement
Of my beloved crank handle.

Something was wrong
Mechanical things go wrong
I had heard

Looking about
I saw not the welcome to the circle
Smiles.
Instead,
My family's faces were laughing

I briefly considered jumping up and down

On the immobile crank
But what if that
Didn't work?

At that moment
If the Earth had opened
I would have gone
Willingly

I lived beyond that day in spite
Of the immovable crank
And
laughing family faces.

Vow after vow
I made that day
Redemption would be sweet
Someday.

Was never to be.

My dad bought an
Electric Ice cream maker.
The mechanical maker
Had indeed met its maker.
I was told

You know making
Ice cream at home
was never the same.
The ice cream somehow
Had lost its personality

All these many decades later
I have not cranked the
Crank of an ice cream maker
My redemption in limbo.

Nor have I had a spoonful
Of sweet summer
Ice cream
Homemade.

# Freedom When I was Ten

When I was ten
I had a bike of my very own.
O, I went far and wide on my bike,
A remarkable feat for a girl.
Sometimes all the way to Green Valley
Ice Cream Parlor.
I never went in.

A short distant away I was free of
Watchful eyes peering from our front porch.
I was free, just my bike and me.
Always fun to ride up over the railroad
And down again.

Once I was privileged to go on an errand.
All the way to the meat market for
2 pounds of round, ground twice.
It was an easy trip on my bike
Because of the basket on the front was
Just the right size.

One day my freedom wrecked.
A delivery truck backed over my
Bike and I barely escaped to the curb
Only skinning my knee.
My bike lay crumpled under the wheel, the driver
Looked at the bike.
And me sitting on the curb crying.

The truck owner gave my dad a check for my wrecked
Bike.
He bought a swing set for my younger brothers and sisters.
I was too big to swing; I could only push others.

I went everywhere on my bike.
Hair blowing in the
Wind, my spirits free.
When I was ten

From Nancy's Days

# Flow

Time claims its
Due.
Life sustains its
Hope.
Faith extends its
Proof.

Set apart at ends
To drift afar
Unguided, unheralded
And undeserving
Of
More.

Time to pass without
Measure.
Distance unclaimed
Nor the
Matter.

Things held once
And
Often
Are not to travel.

Peace of future.
Claims forgiven.
Alone now
And forever.

Ponder no longer
Not the matter,
Not the could
Have been.
Not the past.
And its destination
Flow is a traveler
Neither known nor cared.

So tears freeze?
Do broken hearts
Flee?

Flow answers all.
Flow to the edge,
To the end.
But
Not before me.

# A Hopeful Plea

Nancy Reifke

Deafness resounds inside
My pen held tight.
The wordless music
Constitutes my flight.

Fearful am I if frankness
Which might hurt those I love
But a note to put my music to
Would turn darkness to lightness alone.

So, to each of my loved ones
Know that these words are you.
My heart sings the music
But without words that's tough to do.

In a note home
October 1966

# Best I Know

I love you best I know
Today and yesterday.
Tomorrow yet to show.

I meet your train
Today and yesterday.
Don't ask me to explain.

I love you best I know
Today and yesterday.
Tomorrow yet to show.

I meet your eyes
Today and yesterday.
They don't tell lies.

I love you best I know
Today and yesterday.
Tomorrow yet to show.

# No. 225-HLSR

My guess is she
Will never know her full
Height.
How could she?

Limbs, fixed
In a bent way,
Forever kinked
At every joint.

An exception,
Her proud jaw is
set and confident
Eyes fixed and self-assured.

Her charger, a color of dark mahogany,
Differs greatly in stature.
He is tall, straight of limb
Shoulders
Muscled, flanks slabbed.
-Correct
By every equine measure.
All speaks of training ethic.

He is her horse
To show and
to win.

Winning is overcoming.
To win is trying your best.
To win is internal
And limitless.

Now, the showground.
No. 225 and other hopefuls.
The crowd silent.

Others and I
Witness her near Herculean effort
To walk,
Leading her pampered horse toward their fate.
The judge does
Her walk-around,
Smiles and releases
Each contestant one by one
To the line up.

The girl's
Return
Seems less difficult.

Does she know?

The announcement is made.

First place.
No. 225
An engraved belt buckle is the prize.

The exit.
She seems taller now,
No mistake-
No. 225 is the winner
Houston Livestock Show and Rodeo
Special Olympics.

# Conversation Lost

Days past conversation served
At diners, street corners and porches
Replaced with TV talk shows and Internet blogs.

Entire communities and neighborhoods sat on
Summertime front porches, shaded by
A giant elm tree,
Or at Sunday's dinner table,
Or astride corral fences, and conversed.

A governing protocol attached to all conversations.
Elders spoke in questioning tones of contemplation.
Bread winners spoke of politics, organized labor and
The next President.

Wives, less conspicuous,
Talked of recipes, children
And other wives.

Teens twitched to be free.
While understanding their ticket out
Was respect and silence.

Children flitted about like butterflies,
Sometimes underfoot, often quietly misbehaving,
Always self interested.

Still, conversations continued by one and all.

Today, seldom is simple conversation
conducted from neighbor to neighbor.
Now, people are prisoners of their garage door openers,
Powerless of individual thinking or strength of voice.

Conversation lost.

# JANUARY 6, 1984

*"Early, too soon to tell."*
Dark fear,
No morning sunlight yet.
It should be dark.
I am afraid.
You know where to go,
Where you should be,
So get there.
Not to be late, late is
Something everyone else does.
Not you.
Work at all costs,
Work has given you substance,
A
Reason for being.
Where were you before work?
Work divides the people
Those who work hard get
Their share of the 'ol American pie

Those who don't work get
Nothing,
Or nothing they care to admit.
Work, because that's all you have.
It feeds your mind
And
Rewards your soul.
It
Extends the purpose that
Allows you to have
What you have.
You've earned it.

Why work?
Why not become a non-worker?
To lay in the sun
On a grassy knoll
On a clear day
And
Enjoy what you feel.
Without regard for the
Price of doing nothing.

# Middle Earth

Rush to Middle Earth
is not torrential, at first.
drops of hope splattered
the brain like raindrops on a windshield.

Always the same, the brain interrupts
asking, is there more?

More life, other life experiences
searching me?

Dare I open my heart to see?
or will my eyes capture only
the familiar?

I see the middle of life.
Behind the earth filled space
of time past.

Now is unsatisfactory.
It only is propelled
beyond return.

Ahead, ambition calls
To fulfill wants shut away,
stagnate and sour.
Sadly, not forgotten.

Selfish human spirit laden
with covetousness.

Internally, warning comes to mind
My foothold on reality is giving away.
In angry disbelief I curse.
With outstretched arms I pray
for guarantees of safety.

Heart pounding,
Knowing, the next step must be
Taken.
Now.
The neon bright warning of giving away past
bursts in the mind saying-
Cannot go back.

Middle earth is a grown-up place.
Past are the indecisions of youthful exuberance.
Comfort is the only goal.

To have achieved the prescription of
society.
Tearfully distance our dreams, our best selves,
the essence unique to us and latch the box.

Shamefully, arrogantly you unlatch
the future.
You step toward the abyss and next,
To leave the safe, comfortable middle.
Ascending to personal fulfillment.

Frightening to leave grasping dreams.
Dreams of informed intelligence, ambition,
and a simple life.
An uneasy truce at best.

# Behind Her Eyes

Not a single event missed.
Never.
Behind her eyes
Dwelt the custos of forever hope.

Respecter of thought
She managed others
To set her coarse.

Behind her eyes
She conveyed that which
Is heard universally
Without a word
Spoken.

Grandmother- in a truly Irish way,
"Eyes that set ones wits to work."

Grandfather- in a scholarly voice,
She will never "suffer
The torments of Tantalus."

As an infant,
And now
Behind her eyes
Foretold of never being denied.

Never.

# Y-O Gang

The gang, both of us
Defy a balance of nature.

Youth, always eager
And
Secure in knowledge learned
And
Curiosity unrequited.

Old, reluctant
To force antique
Perceptions.
Although wizened,
A mental fissure exists.

Youth easily builds
A bridge
Connecting childlike folly
With fact forgotten.

Here deep in meaningful
Conversation
The gang
Discusses a little lizard
Staring from a leafy branch
Just outside the kitchen window.

Oh, did you know
Dinosaurs could
Eat tractors?